...Before Being Found
by Love Again

August · 20, 2001~.

Nine Letters
to a Dead Man...

...Before Being Found
by Love Again

Dear Behly: To an
old and dear friend, from
past journeys... with
fond memory and high
regard.

Mar Sulaika Ochs

with faith in
magic and love

HARA
PUBLISHING GROUP

Published by
Hara Publishing
P.O. Box 19732
Seattle, WA 98109
(425) 775-7868

LCCN: 00-111539
ISBN: 1-883697-06-9

10 9 8 7 6 5 4 3 2

Editor: Vicki McCown
Cover and Graphic Design: Scott Carnz
Cover Art: Peter Paul Ochs

Printed in Korea

To: "Him"...

...who takes me to the eternity of Capistrano...every day.

Forward

The courage required for loving another may not be fully understood until we stand amid the eternal ways with death, bidding farewell to our beloved. The exquisite agony of grief is shrouded in longing and a raw awareness of the meaning of aloneness. Fortunately, the last three decades have produced a plethora of information, books, and movies on this part of life called grieving. How many of us have raced to a bookstore or library to read anything and everything about this desolate land we have found ourselves in? For some it provides the comfort of knowing the new territory has a road map or that others have traveled here and have survived. Yet, there is more to this journey than loss and grief. There is the important aspect of mourning.

Mourning has been traditionally defined as the cultural and/or public display of grief through one's behavior. Yet, Mar's narrative invites us to look at mourning as both the conscious and unconscious process that allows one to traverse this territory of grief toward a world without our beloved. The first task of mourning is the undoing of the ties that bind us to our beloved one. It is a time of internal focus seeking every corner of our heart and soul recalling, reexperiencing, swimming in the emotional wake of separation. As Mar reflects, "I wander the moors of my soul like a ghost searching for Heathcliffe. Abelard and Tristan. And You. Dear Peter..."

The second task is to begin the necessary revision of the world we use to know and to begin to adapt the roles, skills, and behavior that will help us develop a new identity without our partner. Mar begins this journey when she comes to this realization, "Then, one day in Whistler, I looked at that box of ashes and I thought, it's time. Time to put you at rest. To put you away. To start a new thread in my own magic carpet."

The third and final task requires us to move into the new world and reinvest in people, roles, hopes, beliefs, goals—knowing all the while that each step takes us away from our beloved and toward a future where our partner does not exist. And, yes, perhaps "being found by love again."

Mourning is not a road or path with predictable stops along the way. It does not follow a set course or have a predictable timetable. It is a process that weaves its way in and out of the myriad of feelings, desires, longings and dreams that have created who we were, how we loved, who we are and where our destination will be. Mar takes us into this intimate process which on the one hand affirms the uniqueness of grief, and on the other hand demonstrates the undulating experience of mourning that is a necessary require- ment for us all. To love requires courage. To grieve requires stamina. To mourn requires self-compassion. To love again requires the faith that can only come from having once been touched by love.

Mar's unique prose coupled with her ability to stand revealed to the reader provides an opportunity for us all to begin to understand this process called mourning. Peter's paintings bring to life the stories she tells just as his dying has helped create the storyteller. The story itself allows us to understand that even after death the rela- tionship lives on.

Jessica Easton
Psychotherapist
MA., PhD (Cand.)

Introduction

A love poem by Johann Goethe is tucked away in an artist's memory for thirty-six years until he meets a young writer he names "Sulaika." Not knowing why and not remembering the origin of this name, he tells her simply, wistfully, "...that is who you are...."

In 1985, when I met artist Peter Paul Ochs, I was thirty years old. He was twenty-four years older. When he died in my arms, I was thirty-nine.

It's the way he looked back into my soul that night we were introduced. I still feel my body tumble down a black, velvet tunnel with that exchange. In an instant I knew I was embraced by destiny; there was a reason I had to know him and he to know me.

Five years later, on Valentine's Day 1990, oncologists told us he had leukemia. We were preparing for a ten-week one-man art exhibit sponsored by the Canadian Embassy overseas.

Instead, we planned our marriage that February night. My wedding gift to Peter was to legally change my name to Sulaika. I still did not know who this was and neither did he.

Four years later, I woke up to find Peter dying beside me.

They say that love changes you, but that death changes you completely. My love story with Peter Paul Ochs is a profound journey of a man and a woman holding hands and then having to let go. Of being one with another and then being one in solitude. Of being one alone, but then being found by a new love, a new alchemy where the ordinary is transformed into the extraordinary.

It is in this tribute that I say goodbye to Peter, our life, my memories. In so doing, I release his precious name for me: his name I grew into because "...that is who you are...."

That is who I was.

It is my hope, my wish, that these letters by a widow will help other widows, other mates, understand how we proceed from one place of love to another place of love. Perhaps because they too will take this profound journey. It happens. It's happening to me.

Marlène Ochs
March 6, 1999.

**Spanish Banks, British Columbia,
Summer 1989**

*Returning from life in Greece, Peter has his fingers crossed for us
to have good luck.*

Letter 1

The First Six Months

Dear Peter,

I don't know what to do. Do without you. I feel dead. I cry like my skin is on fire. A shower feels like knife blades. My skin aches for you. I can't be touched. I need to be touched. I want to be touched. By you. Where are you?

Please, please be there, somehow. Somehow not dead. All of this, please be a dream. But it is not. And I howl and keen, wrap my arms around my body, rock, rocking myself into sheer exhaustion, not sleep. A thousand rocking tears finally put me out.

It seems that my pillow is wet, day and night. I cannot accept that your smile will never again hold me, that your arms will never find me in the middle of the night sleep, that your kiss will never again awake me with the morning sun.

How can I go on? Why do I want to?

I have to tell you a story. Jerry and Bette invited me to take care of their seaside home and their dog, Casey, while they went to Europe. I was so grateful to hold this warm body as she slept. A dog. I needed to hold this animal. I thought this would amuse you because you know my ambivalence about dogs. But I held that dog as if it were a life raft. A life raft I needed because you were not there.

One bad night when a seaside wind was whistling through their forest, you finally did come. Late. I heard you on the deck. That quiet pacing you make. It's you, I know it's you. The sea spray sound finds my ears, my feet tickle, my toes rustle out of the down covers. It's your breathing, I can hear it.

Your smell. I can smell your cedar smell after you've been carving. My nostrils quiver as memory beckons.

My legs swing to the side of the bed. I am nude. I can only sleep so my own arms wrap around me, so I can touch my own skin, so that I know I am still here, still real. All of the rest of day-to-day life is too surreal. I travel the hall of wood and walls in a daze to get to you. My feet float through the carpet.

I'm at the window, but you are not there. I don't see you, but I know I heard you. It's dark. I lie on the couch with my spine against the back of it, so I can feel the hug and hold of something. I whisper to myself, "It's only my imagination."

Oh, my heart breaks. I feel like a big, crystal vase that has shattered into a thousand shards, glued back together by the process of breathing. Me: it's still a vase, it can still hold water. But it's a vase with cracks.

The couch back feels like you, just for a moment. There is a sound. A quiet, rustling sound. I am so tired. I turn my head to hear it. And then, I feel the soft plaid of your shirt, the cool denim of your jeans. My breath stops. I don't dare to breathe in again. You are there. My head is on your lap.

I make not one move, for fear of shaking awake what surely must be a dream. But I am wrong. It IS you. I feel your hand on my head, stroke my hair, touch my tears. Across my cheek, just once. Your fingers, strong, beautiful, whisper by my eyelids soaked with wet. I seem to cry without crying, holding my breath in so as not to shake the fragile space of the moment.

Hot tears finally fall, jubilant. You've come back.

After thousands of hours of lonely fear, your touch tells me, I am home.

Sulaika as Odalisque, 1993

When your partner dies, the very first thing missing is touch. All things sensuous, anything reminding you of life is suddenly irretrievably gone.

Letter 2

The Next Six Months

Dear Peter,

I can't breathe in this life alone. The days are too long. Too short. Too hot. Too cold. Too much. Too little. Too calm. Too crazy. No visitors. Not enough visitors. Sleep is too painful. Waking is worse. It's twelve noon. Have a martini. It's 4 p.m. and six more. Alone. Leave me alone.

It's seven and I haven't eaten. Food tastes like cardboard. Water burns down my throat. Six olives in a glass is better. It's dark. The garden beckons. Your garden. I don't go out. Then I do. The dirt you lovingly nurtured shouts for your touch. It doesn't want mine. I pick dahlias in the moonlight. It's better that way. It's the dead time.

I sink into the ground, curled up in a ball, flowers by my side. Things are dying. It is fall. There is no sound. My cries have no sound. My cries have been neutered dry. This is silly. Go to bed. I stumble back, out of it, giggling and crying.

That night, drunk, I have a dream.

A beautiful grove of cedar trees rings a small green park with lush lawns. The entrance has a cobble walk and it invites me to come in. I smile. From a distance, oh my God! I see you! I'm about to run to you, when a phone rings. It's insistent, and right beside me. I am caught in a dilemma. Do I run to you, or do I answer the phone?

You smile. Your arms are extended, waiting for me to join you. I pick up the phone but look at you. I'll find out who it is, and then I will ask them to wait.

But they won't let me get off the line. I sputter and try to break away, my feet try to move toward you, but they are stuck in place. Your smile is still there, but the image of you begins to fade. I cannot get off the phone! Please, I'll be right back I shout at them! But they won't let me go!

I simply cannot get to you. I rustle in the covers. The last image is your smile. I am shocked as I wake. You and the lush garden are not really there. I cry for what feels like all my life. Days pass. It becomes winter.

Then something happens.

Bobby "O" Osborne calls out of the blue from Saskatoon. A remarkable conversation ensues. I have to tell you what we talked about, because I'm scared and I don't know what to do now.

"Come and work with me," he says, matter of fact.

"What...?" I answer.

"I need you. I need a good producer."

"Robert, I'm not ready."

"Come on, how long is it now?"

"Six months, two days..."

"It's time you came back to work," he insists.

"I said, I'm not ready."

"Yes, I think you are."

"No! I think I'm not!"

He's pushing. I am angry. I'm not the pit bull television producer I once was.

Gentle years as the artist's wife, as your partner have softened me. I want him to go away.

"Just come for an interview," he persists.

"To Regina? In November?"

"You need to come back to the real world, Mar."

"Robert...I can't."

There's a long pause. Should have known he'd save his slam dunk to be used at a point of exhaustion. Mine.

"How much are those cancer bills you have to pay in Texas?"

I lost it. Started to cry. In our last months together, I was buying groceries on my Visa card. Bobby O manages to jostle a memory of the M.D. Anderson Clinic cancelling a $450 X-ray for us. Might as well have been for forty-five hundred dollars at the time.

"Just come for an interview. I know this is the right thing."

Well, you know what he is like. I told him I would think about it. I told him I would call back in a week. I didn't.

Shortly after that, I was looking for something. I came across my diary with the dream where you beckon and smile while I am on the phone trying to get off it so that I can be with you.

Months later, I now know what it means.

You have to stay on the phone, Sulaika. That's what you were telling me.

And so I am going for an interview for a job half way across the country, away from our house, our garden, our life. Then I remind myself, that there is no "us" anymore.

There's just me.

Landscape: "Bridging Life and Death" Series, 1992

With over fifty paintings, Peter began this project six months
before diagnosis of cancer. The moods and colours are ominous,
dark, mysterious. By the time he completed "Bridges," they, like
him, had gone through the convolutions of emotion: from toxic pain
in blacks to the moving conclusion of release in sky blues and pinks.
"The Oak Street Bridge" in watercolour is the most ethereal.

Letter 3

Let the Morphine Begin

Dear Peter:

I remember the day you talked to Shakespeare. At least that's what you said at the time. I never doubted one word. It was when Dr. Rob Lehman came to the house to introduce us to Morpheus, the God of Dreams. I remember this story because it makes me laugh and smile when I cry with the pain. Other partners who have lost their mate like to hear this story too. They get it.

Two weeks earlier you hesitated. Didn't want to start with the morphine. We both knew it was a signal; a signal for the end. But you were in such pain, it was necessary. Dr. Lehman was a just few years younger than I. You, the much older man in our lives. We were both like your kids that day we discussed drug maintenance.

It was that day you chose to do it. You asked us to help you die. Rob and I were sitting on each side of our king size-bed, you in the middle, holding court. Your grey hair was long, still a lion's mane; your blue eyes ice-cold and hurting. Your hands crossed gracefully in front of you.

"There must be a way that you can do this, to help me," you said.

"What are you talking about?" I asked.

"You know what I am talking about," you said, angry.

At first I could not understand the words that followed and then when I understood, I couldn't believe them. I snapped. From somewhere, I don't know where, I was cool and calm. I always could match you guts for guts when I had to.

"Don't you ever ask me to do that again," I said simply.

Rob looked at me, at you. "I've never been asked to do that as a doctor before, Peter. I..."

"Rob, don't," I said, turning back to you. "We love you and we are not going to do this. We will do anything within our power to help you, but not that. And by the way, it is really unfair for you to ask."

You and I locked stares. This was the supreme test that you levelled at me, at our love, on our path.

But anger at our betrayal created a solution. Morphine.

On that day, when I brought the brown bottle home with a specific spoon for measuring the clear, sticky liquid, I felt like an alchemist. This magic potion would deliver you from exhausting, sword-cutting pain. I was grateful and terrified.

You insisted on administering it yourself. You wanted to be in charge, in touch, and in control of what would happen. You fell into sleep, as I touched your brow, wiped your forehead, and kissed your cheek.

Forty minutes later, I brought in lunch and stopped in my tracks. You were sitting up in bed. Your eyes were sparkling, alert, more aware than I had seen in four weeks.

By that time on our journey, I could swerve out of the way of some punches our uninvited houseguest, leukemia, would pack. Cancer is as disruptive as a drunk neighbour who won't leave your house until he's smashed some furniture. I looked at you.

"So...," I ventured, "how do you feel?"

"I've got to get out of here," you said, your face feverish, excited.

I stared. You hadn't been out of bed for nine weeks.

"Oh? You're feeling that strong are you?"

But you ignored me, gobbling down your soup like you had never seen food. Your thirst for life rejuvenated.

I stared again. You hadn't been eating for weeks, our supply of BOOST, the only thing you could stomach, was down to the last three containers.

"So, what, uh...what happened in there the last hour?" I asked, indicating your head.

"Well, we've got LOTS to do today," you said with emphasis. "I've just been talking to Shakespeare."

Like you were just talking to Ed, the mailman.

I stared again.

My God. You were. I could only humour you as I sat on the edge of the bed.

"And, so, uh…what are you two guys, ahem…gonna do?"

Looking back at me as if I had two heads, you diplomatically informed me, while wiping the last of the soup off your beard.

"Well…the first thing we have to do…," you said looking up, "…is…reinvent the coffee machine."

I stared. The button in my head said "cry" but the button on my heart said "laugh." I did the latter, grateful you were out of pain and apparently having a good time.

When I closed the door that day, I thought of Dr. Lehman holding me in a bear hug the day you asked us to help you die. He was upset, in tears. "He was so mad at me, but I just can't do it, Sulaika."

"He didn't mean to get angry at you, Rob. He loves you. He's just so sick."

Now when I tell people the story, when I remember it for myself, I recall the Greek myth of the two brothers: Hypnos, the God of Sleep, and Thanatos, the God of Death, who take us to bed every night and fight over who will win.

Only Morpheus, the son, the God of Dreams, can hold us in between the two who fight over us.

On that day Morpheus held you, I was able to sleep that night, for the first time.

Thanatos and Hypnos could only watch.

The Sun Canoe, January 1994.

Peter's last painting, unfinished and yet very finished. I used this
in our morphine meditations. I would say "...put your pain in the
head of the canoe, Peter, let the canoe sail away with your pain,
because that's why you painted it..."

Letter 4

Our First Anniversary

Dear Peter:

Marking the first wedding anniversary, that first year without you. Oh, my dear, where are you...?

I've invited Chris and Sheila, Shirley and Roy, Doreen and Barry, and John and Laura over for a summer dinner of ginger salmon. It would only have been our fourth, not a long time to have been married, no. Too short. But wonderfully full, rich. When people ask me how long we were together, it's an easy answer: "...about four hundred years..."

The sun shines for us. I am wearing yellow. I have been cooking all day. The balcony beckons with your beloved geraniums, which we called "geronimos." I look out at the blue-black water and recall my dream earlier in the day; a cruel joke.

In the dreamscape of endless flowing sunshine, I was getting married again. I looked into my reflection and said to myself, "To Peter?" You were certainly present in spirit, but I never did see this man I was to marry. I was happy again. Happy to share my life with someone. Our house was in a lush valley of rolling hills. I had a lot to do, kept looking for someone to help me finish final details, but I could find no one. I was doing it alone, but I was content.

The big, glorious house was suddenly dark and there you were, just looking at me, into me.

There was love in your eyes, like that day we found the wounded nightingale in Greece. Something so tender was lit inside of you, it caught my breath.

In the dream, I was trying to explain to you how happy I was. All you did was look at me and listen. I was so joyous! But when I awoke to find it only a dream, I wept. It was me letting go of you in a most definite and dramatic way. How could I do that? I wrote in my journal.

The reality, dear Peter, is there is no one. No one's been waiting in the wings. I have to put my upset feelings away, soon. Our guests will be over to celebrate life that goes on living, remembering you, the man we miss who is dead.

"I'll never forget that time I came over in the winter. You'd just come back from Texas and he was very weak," recalls old Chris, "and he had one big log in the fireplace and he lit one piece of paper, and I laughed and said, 'Peter...if you actually get that thing going, I will kiss your ass in front of the Post Office.'"

We all giggle, relieved. You were an expert woodsman. It was just so tender to remember how vulnerable you suddenly had become. We laughed because we loved you, love remembering you.

Shirley, who knew the value of expensive, beautiful things, said, "Those are striking earrings."

I touched my earlobes. "They were last year's gift. He had asked me what I wanted and stupidly I said to him, 'I'd like your friend to make me something.'

"I was referring to the jeweller, Karl Stittgen. I had no idea what I was asking. I just remember Peter being very thoughtful about it for a few days. No wonder; they cost more than the house you are sitting in right now!"

But we did go to Stittgen's, I tell our friends. Like stepping inside what I would imagine a Fabergé egg to be; it was elegant and golden. We couldn't afford this stuff! My first clue should have been that not one price tag was visible.

"Unpretentious as always, Peter was in plaid shirt and faded jeans. They'd known each other since the 1950s and chatted comfortably. Stittgen pulled out a tray of the most glorious creations: earrings in ebony with gold flecks, gold globes, gold chunks, gold everywhere. I felt like a kid in a candy store, saying, 'Oh, I like that...oh that is so nice...Peter look at this!...'

"The telephone rang. Stittgen went into an alcove to answer it.

That was my chance. I saw a card discreetly tucked in by the corner of his desk with price listings. I peered down at it...

"I thought my heart was going to bounce off the floor. I looked up. Peter stared back. He'd known the prices before we got there. That's why he'd been so pensive weeks before. My eyes began to water. I suddenly felt selfish and greedy.

"'We have to get out of here,' I whispered. But he just looked at me and smiled.

"We couldn't spend that kind of money anymore. Not with cancer treatments in Houston every six months.

"'...Come on,' I urged, 'tell him anything. I changed my mind, we can't afford this stuff....' But it was too late. Stittgen returned. And his cool, calculated stare matched my frozen, scared one.

"Only Peter was in command as he stared quietly at us.

"'You've set aside three pairs that you like, Sulaika,' said Stittgen. 'Have you decided which ones you like best?'

"'Ah...well...actually, you know the very first ones I saw? The ones with just one tiny, little speck of gold in the centre? Those. I like those best.'

"Peter had his hands in his lap. 'No, she really likes these,' he said, retrieving the biggest gold globes set in ebony on the tray. I had to choke back a sound in my throat.

"We could have used the money in a thousand more important ways, but here he was buying me something beautiful, expensive from his old friend. Something my child's heart really wanted.

"'Done!' said the gleeful merchant and I blinked as I reached for Peter's hand. He squeezed back.

"'She deserves them,' he said, 'and more.'

"'But...'

"'He really wants to buy them for you, my dear' said the jeweller quietly.

"And so," I tell Sheila and Chris, Shirley and Roy, Doreen and Barry, John and Laura, "I happily wear them. They make me feel like a queen. He was my king."

"What you had so young in your life, what you two had together, few others ever get in an entire lifetime," said Chris.

A hush fell over the table.

I know.

Raven Stealing the Sun: Rosewood and Carnelian

Peter made jewellery, specialising in exotic woods. His favourite piece, a gift to me, reminds me of his final, graceful release from life. The Carnelian is the August birthstone.

Letter 5

The Day Our World Changed

Dear Peter,

I am having a breakdown.

I can't do this anymore. Go on, I mean.

I...just...simply...can't. Another session with grief therapist, Jessica, scotch-taping my soul back together again. It just isn't working. She holds me in her arms. I cry so hard I don't make a sound, rocking back and forth unable to stop shaking. After two years, the past still collides with the present. Every four weeks.

Death lives in me, Peter. I allowed it to move into me after it left you. How did that happen? It found a place to grow inside of me. It is heavy and black and I cannot release its gorilla grip on my heart and my guts. I wish I could break forever and be done with it. I don't want to feel anything anymore. I want to die.

I wander the moors of my soul like a ghost, searching for Heathcliffe, Abelard, and Tristan. And you. Dear Peter, there are days I simply cannot move. Or breathe. Or try. Or eat. Or sleep. Or sit. Why didn't I know this would happen? How could I?

I remember that day in October. Our last October.

We knew it then, sensed it, refused to say it out loud. But saying it out loud to a therapist two years later doesn't make it comprehensible. How, how do I figure this out?

1993. I remember coming back on the ferry to Gibsons Landing. I remember your cool blue eyes meeting me at our front door, the one you painted purple. How different you looked. How at peace. "Let's go for a walk," you said.

Frozen fear hit my stomach like a punch, as I heard your voice. Something had happened while I was gone. In the quiet without me you had worked out some deal after a wrestling match with the gods.

I reached for your hand, but it was already reaching for mine. Yours was warm, secure. I know now, you were taking care of me. Taking care of how you were going to tell me.

The blue-black of the water stared at me, daring me to breathe. The blue-black knew I had to summon the courage to ask. I could only hold my breath until it returned to a steady beat. You patiently, gently waited.

"It didn't work," you said.

You squeezed my hand.

"What do you mean?" I asked, shaking. I knew what you meant. I squeezed back. "Tell me."

I can't breathe, waiting for your answer. I choke back a guttural sound that wants to escape to become a scream. You squeeze my hand again.

"The cells didn't take in the bone marrow for the transplant. It's not going to work."

I stop. I look up. My eyes are full. Your eyes lean down. We wrap around the other's winter jacket and hold. Hold and wait and rock and hold.

"Don't let me go," I whisper.

You don't for a very long time....

"How long do we have?"

"They don't know."

"What do we do?'

"The best we can."

We're down to the blue-black water's edge. Something precious holds us. Too precious a moment to even cry. We stand arm in arm, looking at the blue-black of the sea. Deathly quiet, as if God holds us in His palm and we bathe in some kind of warmth, knowing we aren't going to be there long.

Like your painting of Adam and Eve and the Serpent. We are leaving the garden. We are banished.

There are no words.

Only touch.

Just your hand holding mine holding yours.

Holding onto life as hard as we can.

02/07/91

Gibsons Landing, 02-07-91.

The blue-black of Howe Sound as seen by Peter from our living room balcony where he would paint during his last six months. Forever relentless in changing moods, this water vision would hold us and haunt us.

Letter 6
The Day You Died

Dear Peter,

Our last twenty-four hours I will never forget. A profound journey. We never know when that gun goes off as a signal to us, but we will always remember.

It was April 30 and it had been days of three-hour grabs for sleep, intermingled with constant trips to pharmacies, grocery stores, friends' houses to pick up this and that. My dad had just died two days earlier after a sudden heart attack. The news flung you into anguish and despair.

"I'm the one who is supposed to die!" you cried, devastated.

The nurses had been coming once a week, thank God for them. They were so kind. All of it became an unreal, surreal movie trailer of moments glued together badly.

You were incontinent and, oh, how humiliated you were! I was changing sheets, laundering every other day to keep up. Ardith came over with her massage table and managed to take away the pain in your pelvic bone. Midnight sometimes she would come and stay and hold pressure points until the wee, small hours.

But on that day, I needed, desperately, somehow to be alone. Our hairdresser, Jeanette, came over, happy to relieve me. Her big, warm body hugged me close and told me to go to a movie. I saw Six Degrees of Separation but I wasn't really there.

The only thing I know for sure is that I wasn't with death, our uninvited guest from hell, and yet he managed to sneak into the theatre and gloat at me.

In the movie house, suddenly, for no reason, I peed in my pants. My bladder, like yours, released itself involuntarily. I ruefully acknowledged our sympathetic pain connection. I watched the movie as if it were my last meal, so hungry was I for anything but being taunted by death's bad breath like a cauldron over me.

When I arrived home at nine-thirty, I wasn't really sure what I'd just seen at the movies, separated as I was. I was just thankful to be away. Jeanette was reading in the living room. The lights were warm and low. I asked if you had eaten. She smiled, sad.

"He had a little chicken broth, but not much. And he was lying there, with his long grey hair tucked behind his ears, so I asked him, 'Would you like me to cut your hair, Peter?' And you know what he said?"

I started to smile; I could feel a "Peter Moment" about to surface.

"He says, 'No, I like to have my ears showing!'"

When she hugged me goodbye, her eyes filled with tears. We said nothing; there was nothing to say. I still didn't really know. But when I walked into our bedroom, I knew something.

You had gotten yourself to sit upright for the first time in weeks. Your face. It held the full power of life as you stared at me, wordless. There was a shine around you. At the time I thought it was the bedside lamp; but no, it was something otherworldly. Consciously, I could only react with sudden, intense action.

"I'll be right there," I said quickly, disrobing not wanting to miss one moment of time. When I crawled in nude beside you, I remember hugging my body into your back and reaching for your hand, but it suddenly went straight up into the air.

You said something in your mother tongue. I listened. Something about drinking water. You said, "...that's right, you don't speak German..."

"Sweetheart, why do you have your hand in the air?"

"I'm waiting for the gun to go off."

"What gun?"

I remembered that you were a long distance runner as a student at the university. Minutes, taking forever, passed.

My left hand reached up to hold your right arm. My fingers pressed into your delicate wrist.

"Darling, while we're waiting for that gun...why don't you put your arm down? It must be getting awful tired."

Slowly, along with my arm guiding yours, you lowered it. And there our hands held onto each other for the entire night.

I curled my body into yours, my chest holding your spine, frail, small, tender. You had gone from father, lover, husband, to son. I kissed your back once, twice, again and again.

Your voice was soft, clear. "Peter loves Sulaika."

"Sulaika loves Peter."

Our last shared words. Our last words to each other.

The next morning, your life ended.

It was the rasping, death rattle breathing that first awakened me, startled me. Startled me even more than the fact that we had not moved an inch away from each other's body, our last moments of life as one were spent as one. In the same curled position, all through the ten hours of sleep, we went through that dark, subconscious place we dreaded. That place where we would part company. Forever. Our hands once intertwined, would never, could never, touch again.

As innocent as we were when we married, when we knew you were going to die, when we knew our last days were precious and few, we still went forward together, together until the very last moment we could not.

My dear, sweet love, when I think of that day, those last twenty-four hours, I am so grateful to have been touched and held by you. By love.

Portrait of Peter Paul Ochs

Just Married, July 1990, in Vancouver, and painting. Cast bronze sculpture of Bucephalus, Alexander the Great's horse, in background.

Letter 7

Four Years Later

Dear Peter:

I'm mad at you. Mad at you for leaving me. Mad at you for loving me. Mad at you for choosing me. I used to be mad at you for not taking me with you to die. We HAD talked about it. But here it is, four years after your death, and I'm still alone, still unable to have a life rich, without you in it. Without someone in it. What's wrong with me?

I am listening to "our" song for the first time since you died. For years, I could not bear to hear Rimsky-Korsakov's "Scheherazade" without going into a tailspin of tears. Tears that would only end in exhausted sleep. But I listen to it now because I really want to exorcise you out of MY bone marrow. As if listening to this symphonic love story will shake me awake and away.

I shudder to think that your love does not comfort me now.

It is but a memory. And a memory cannot scrub my back, hold me at three in the morning, or tease me into a smile when I am cranky.

I'm supposed to get angry. All the grief books agree on that. Once I do, I'm supposed to feel better. But I feel betrayed. I feel betrayed because no one else understands this except you. And you are not here.

Did you know that most of our married friends never call me anymore? Apparently, dinner for nine doesn't work.

Shocked, I catch myself hiding. People ask how long you've been gone. I say automatically, "About two years." No! It's four! Some part of me does not want to admit reality.

As time goes on, I'm not a widow any longer, but a single woman. Again. Now I'm a threat. I don't want to be single. I don't want to be a threat. How did that happen?

With you, I knew where I belonged. I had a purpose. My purpose was to be your wife, to love you. I get that. I know how to do that. I'm very good at it. And you loved how I did that. But you're not here and I feel like a crazy person in search of the only other crazy person who "gets me."

Why is this so hard?

Even when I finally buried your ashes a year ago, I thought then that it would be over. It's never over, never going to be over, is it? Because one year later, it's still not. And, two and then three years from now...what?

I buried the remains quietly, privately, on the third anniversary of your death. I had carried that cedar box of your ashes around carefully with every move. It was a sentinel. You were still with me, somehow. How I clung onto that!

Then, one day in Whistler, I looked at that box of ashes and I thought, it's time. Time to put you at rest. To put you away. To start a new thread in my own magic carpet.

When I made that decision, it seemed necessary to do this without family. The ceremony, memorial, ritual had already been done in Stanley Park, by Prospect Point, where we were married.

But there was one person I wanted to have by my side. Someone you'd never even met. Someone I barely knew. Yet, someone whose friendship I treasured beyond all measure.

I met him long before I'd known you. I remember telling him about you; he was curious, pensive about my marrying a man ill with cancer. He just looked soulfully into me when I talked of us. He got it. When you died, he sent me the most poignant card. The thoughtfulness of him startled me. I hadn't told him of your death. I still don't know how he found out. But it struck a chord. His sensitive perception resonated within me.

But that was year ago.

And this is now.

And I want this to be over.

Now.

I want to be firmly ensconced in a new life, with a new rhythm, but my fingers cannot locate a pulse, a heartbeat that is not connected to the past. That is not connected to you.

The one thing I did was go back to school. In the United States. I didn't want to bump into any memories of you.

This new reality was like coming out of a long, dark, sleep. Rejuvenated, but with the hangover of one, big, emotional price tag. That's another thing that makes me mad. While I was taking care of you and cancer, I wasn't taking care of me. Wasn't paying attention.

I worry that I've missed other signals, other messages of life after death. My life, after your death. Important messages about living on without you. No one can tell me anything that helps. It seems I am in this inchoate state, a desert of incomprehensibility. Still.

As I drive to the university, the sun shines bright and clear. My screenplay is as finished as it can be for now and I smile. I notice robins fly past me towards the Communications Building. A sentence leaps into my head.

Wait a minute.

I have started a new life, a new page without you.

Calm sits beside me as I park my car.

The green of the trees is so lush and alive, the sky so blue, the smell of summer hot and sweet.

I stare out for a moment.

How about that.

Greek Still Life Quartet 10-12-1986.

Although one of the four squares is empty, it is surrounded by three other squares filled with colour and life; making it one complete picture.

Letter 8

What If This Man Dies Too?

Dear Peter,

There's this man.

His name is Ward. A big, solid man with hard, old muscles. Been-Around-The-Block-Four-Times Muscles.

I think, I think you would like him. I think he likes you. When he made his first visit and looked at your Raven series of art, he smiled, as if being let into a secret. Our secret. Our secret from the past.

I know one thing.

He really likes me, Peter. When I talk to you, fewer times now in my nightly promenade with your favourite birds at Mallard Point down the street, I feel like you are sitting in the love seat of our garden, tapping your fingers on your faded jeans, looking at me. You are so wise. Twenty-four-years-older wiser than I. Ward is a little younger than you, but still older than I. What do you think?

Sometimes, I get scared. I feel like an orchid, opening, slowly, carefully. A dark thought scorches my memory banks.

What if? What if I only had four years with him too? What if

HE gets cancer?

My mind reels, images flash of you and me. What if Ward and I have to crawl on our bellies and scream at God?

What if I could not take his pain away either? What happens if my heart learns how to race again at every cough? If I fail again? If I am left alone again? If I have to bury another man...again?

I don't want to be in this panic. How do I get out?

Is falling and being in love worth it? Is it worth feeling so much joy my heart feels like it is bathed in golden light? Or so much fear my heart feels trapped by steel claws?

The sound of my cowboy boots – cowgirl boots to you – makes contact with the cement walk. I am impatient to hear confidence in my footfalls.

When I am beside him, inside him, these fears are dispelled.

I think of being with him. Gently my fingers touch the corners of his eyes where his wrinkles are. My lips kiss the edge of that wrinkle pond. That's the test, when I look at him, looking at me, I know.

I know it IS worth it.

At Mallard Point, I continue this discussion with the green heads, but they don't care. They already know how it works.

They waddle and park and sit and swim as I retell the story to myself and to you.

I've gone around the lake three times without thinking of the pain of "what if...." Just thinking of Ward's beautiful, wrinkled face, his blue eyes like aquamarines, glistening when they take me in.

How odd. How wonderful. How wonderfully odd to be at such odds. Odds that once held me back for so long.

You knew, Peter, didn't you? That this would happen? That someone else would find me? And yet, part of you was afraid I would be alone. Another paradox in our life, in our love.

When hands touch, worlds collide, right?

That last year together, holding hands. I think you sensed I would be unable to move forward. And for a long time I didn't and you were right.

When we first decided to marry because you were sick, you said then it wasn't fair to me. Wasn't fair for someone so young to watch their husband die. You knew I'd have a tough time. Like me watching you in your leukemia pain, you could not help me with my own heartache at losing you. Losing us.

Now I sense you smile at me at finding someone else's hand to hold again and my throat closes.

I remember your kiss. But now it is a brief whisper that flies fast past me. That memory of your kiss fades into a sweet cloud of pink candy colours and I am brisk now in my steps back home.

Steps out of the past because I want to get to my phone. To call Ward. To say hello. To talk of nothing and everything.

To hear his voice giggle and spark at hearing mine.

Still Life with 36 Red Roses 2-04-1991.

The flower of love. For my thirty-sixth birthday, Peter gave me
thirty-six red roses. Then he painted them.

Letter 9

I Must Say Goodbye to You

Dear Peter,

Please let me go....

Ward says he cherishes me. This morning he says he's in love with me. That he loves me. I hold onto this big-boned man and I tremble. I realize, startled, how opposite in body type he is from you and that makes me wonder. But his hold is just as secure, there, warm, trusting as yours. What does it mean?

When we made love this morning it was quiet, intense. Our bodies hardly moved as our lips touched. We kiss for a long time, a time not of this world. When we finally opened our eyes to the other, we fell back into the other's arms, drunk with ecstasy, unable even to speak. We swim in eachother's ocean.

Later, I drive to the movies alone, revelling in this newfound warmth that holds me, holds me again, after so long. But I cannot remember what word Ward used to describe me. "You are a - something - kind of woman," he said.

It bugs me that I cannot recall his word. I wrestle with the image of his face and I get frustrated at my memory lapse. He was singling me out, the quality of me, but what was the word?

As I drive, thinking, I see you. Suddenly, it hits me. I start to cry out. Ah! That's what's really bugging me.

I've blocked out this man's word for me because I don't want to believe that this love is really happening. Because if it happens, then you will really be gone.

What we had will really be over.

Then, I laugh. This is absurd! Irrational! Crazy talk! But my tears are hot, my heart flutters recalling black memory. Stop this! Stop it now! I shout at you.

"We've had this conversation, Peter!"

And then I realize.

I am really talking to me.

That calm of Ward settles me again. That calm I get when I think of his eyes looking into me. The image of his face centers my heartbeat. His smile holds me. His voice is excited, eighteen years old again when I call him at work. His sweet laugh.

My body does a sound check with you, a wallet-sized photo of the dream left behind.

Come on, Peter! I want to have that corny experience from the movies where the dearly departed winks or smiles or does some sinister Hollywood thing. From a cloud preferably, to make a point, but of course, you are not here anymore. You are really gone.

A quiet thought. Okay. Do it. Ask him. Now.

Peter, please let me go. It is the very strangest thing to hear myself say this out loud. Please let me go, Peter.

I swallow hard. Is that what I want?

My tears fall, thinking of Ward. Thinking of you. One is dead. The other alive. One has my soul. The other has my heart. You died in my arms. He holds me strong in his.

I think of our "Sulaika" story. People can hardly believe that it is actually true. They love the name, the story. I've retold it hundreds of times and each time people feel their hair stand on end. Delighted.

"...When I met Peter he was fifty-four years old and I was thirty. Almost from the very beginning, he would not call me by my name, 'Mar.' I still remember his eyes blazing into me as he referred to me as 'Sulaika' six months before we began courting.

"I asked who this was, but he said, 'I do not know, but that is who you are.'

"One year later, living together in Greece, then back again in Canada, he would only ever call me Sulaika.

"Then on Valentine's Day 1990, we found out he had leukemia. It was on that day we made plans to marry.

"Quietly, I decided that my wedding gift to him was to legally change my name to 'Sulaika,' not knowing who this was or where the name came from.

"When we moved into our first home, he unpacked what seemed like every book he had ever owned. One night we were in bed.

"He was reading me German stories, then suddenly, joyously, he looked up, his face was beaming and he exclaimed, 'I found Sulaika!'

"It was a poem he had studied when he was eighteen years old. It was written by Johann Goethe to a lover, another writer named Marianne Von Willimar. A poem of love. A poem Peter had tucked away for forty years. A poem deep inside, one he remembered, brought to light the night we met.

"The story is about a man and a woman and the woman's name is...Suleika. It is about a woman who must let go of the man she loves...because he is dying...."

Oh.

My heart breaks to even whisper this story to myself again. But there it is, Peter. I have to let it go, let go of you.

Let go of Sulaika.

By some ironic fluke of the gods turning their ankle on a cloud, it seems that Ward only knows me as Mar because he met me so long ago.

This new love only knows me by the very name you replaced. Like a new king, he replaces the old king.

How strange I would meet someone from so long ago who gently, without knowing it, nudges me out of the life I had with you into a new place, a new future, a new heartbeat.

It's happening. Isn't it?

Once upon a time I was deeply loved by a man who died. A man I loved back so deeply, I can still see and feel his breath on my cheek. But new breath longs to sing inside my lungs as only new breath can.

Peter, I have to tell you one more thing...just so you know it's okay to leave me now.

When Ward and I are together the only sound is the quiet thump-thump of a heartbeat. Ours. In unison. It's as though I know his bones, because they are mine. His arms wrap around me like big, warm paws, so unlike yours, which were tapered and sculpted. He pulls me in close to his chest. I tremble at the feeling of calm, sweet love in my belly. I kiss his hand as it drapes over my waist.

Is it okay to tell you this? I think it must be or I wouldn't be doing so.

You were the love of my life.

My biggest fan.

My best friend. I was so lucky to be touched by love.

By your love.

To have experienced the profound journey we shared, to have been loved like that, means that I can go on. Thank God for you. For the memory of you.

But...

...no sound is more complete, more intimate, more radiant with life itself, than the heartbeat, breathing-in-and-out sound, right beside you of the one you love.

Oil Painting Triptych:
"Sulaika: My Desert Flower" November 1993.

Breaking the spell of this golden name given to me in a golden time,
Peter paints his last portrait of Sulaika.